Brief Casework
with a
Marital Problem

by Lorna Guthrie and Janet Mattinson

978 0901882035

D1741057

INSTITUTE OF MARITAL STUDIES
The Tavistock Institute of Human Relations

First Published 1971

Reprinted December 1972

Second Reprint December 1975

Distributed by

RESEARCH PUBLICATIONS SERVICES LTD.,
Victoria Hall, East Greenwich, London SE10 0RF

Printed in Great Britain by
Headley Brothers Ltd 109 Kingsway London WC2B 6PX and Ashford Kent

PREFACE

This monograph is the third in a series instituted in 1971. It gives an account of a brief piece of work undertaken during the time the two authors (Mrs. A and Miss B in the text) held casework fellowships in the Institute and illustrates the psychological manoeuvres which the couple employed to deal with the anxieties that underlay their marital difficulties. The authors argue the case for brief intensive work at the point the clients bring their crisis.

This publication, *The Marital Relationship as a Focus for Casework* and *Shared Phantasy in Marital Problems* all describe ways in which a psychoanalytic approach can be applied to marital problems and they draw on the theory developed in an earlier book, *Marriage: Studies in Emotional Conflict and Growth* (1960), brought into the series in 1973. The theme of this book is personal growth. Despite increasing criticism of the institution, marriage remains popular. Many young people go into marriage today not talking just of the adjustment they will have to make to each other, but of the opportunity this committed adjustment to a person of the opposite sex will give them for their own personal development—the need for for another to realise parts of themselves. Five cases are described in which the subjects are not different from thousands of others who have not sought help, but failed by themselves to realise their own developmental capacities.

The Marital Relationship as a Focus for Casework discusses some of the basic processes at work in marital interaction and relates these processes to casework undertaken in other settings. *Shared Phantasy in Marital Problems* gives an account of work with two cases, emphasising the collusive and shared nature of the interaction and discusses the use of joint interviews, the two workers meeting husband and wife together.

Marital Interaction and some Illnesses in Children, suggesting a link between a type of marital interaction and certain symptoms in children, portrays another aspect of marital work which has subsequently claimed our attention. The symptoms described are those of encopresis and asthma. Four cases are used to illustrate a tentative approach towards understanding and helping a sick child through working with the marital interaction of his parents.

The Reflection Process in Casework Supervision illustrates our attempt to engage with interactive processes as they are experienced in the supervision and teaching of casework. The thesis that 'the processes at work in the relationship between client and worker are often reflected in the relationship between worker and supervisor', how an awareness of this can be used diagnostically, and a statement of basic theoretical assumptions underlying this thesis, are illustrated by examples taken from tape recording transcripts of seminars for work supervisors.

Marriage and Mental Handicap, first published in 1970 by Duckworth, is the most recent addition to this paperback series. It is the report of a research project on thirty-two on-going marriages in which both partners had been diagnosed as mentally handicapped. The types of marital participation and interaction are studied in an attempt to understand why many of the subjects, considered defective when they were single, were more effective when paired and how they used their commitment to their partner for their own personal development. The method of interviewing shows the use the author made of her casework experience and the excerpts from the tape recordings of these interviews illustrate the importance of listening to clients, whatever their level of intelligence.

The Institute of Marital Studies

CONTENTS

CONTENTS

INTRODUCTION

This record of the casework done with a young couple with marital difficulties is presented as an example of "brief casework" contained in a period of twelve weeks.

The marital department offering help was the Institute of Marital Studies[1] in the Tavistock Centre, London. The two caseworkers assigned to the husband and wife were students, holding casework Fellowships at the Institute for one year. One was a probation officer, and the other, who had been a child care officer, was a tutor in charge of a social work course. Between them they had sixteen years of social work experience.

The case of Mr and Mrs Lorenz was referred to the Institute by a probation officer and is typical of many other cases which find their way to probation departments. Unlike clients who present their marital problems by threatening to desert the children or by seeking help for the disturbed symptoms the children display, unlike those clients who, with an even more despairing cry, break up their families by getting themselves evicted, unlike those whose difficulties in relationships are expressed in somatic illnesses, Mrs Lorenz invoked the representative of the legal system, the probation officer, to make Mr Lorenz, her "bad" husband, better. A department which might reform fitted in well with their shared phantasy[2] that the bad was mainly in him and the good mainly in her. It was probably not chance that the marital difficulties were not expressed more explicitly by Mrs Lorenz in the hospital where she was treated for a thyroid condition, despite the doctor's saying he could not understand why this was so unstable, even after treatment. Clients do seem to use a particular door into a situation of receiving help, which reflects in its public image the way they see their problems being solved.

1 Previously known as the Family Discussion Bureau.

2 See *Shared Phantasy in Marital Problems: Therapy in a four-person relationship.* K. Bannister and L. Pincus. Codicote, 1965.

Although Mr and Mrs Lorenz both had seriously deprived backgrounds and he had a criminal record, they were able to use a type of casework help which refused to support their existing belief that she was almost blameless and that he, in his own words, was "not worth £40 a week". It did, however, give them two other kinds of support. It offered them regular, weekly interviews at a stated time for a known period. Mr and Mrs Lorenz knew how long they had to hold, on their own, any feelings of discomfort which the work roused in them. They also learnt during this time, when they were experimenting with a shift in their relationship, that the two workers would share with them the weight and sadness of the feeling which they helped them to feel and to acknowledge, and then to tolerate.

The account of the work is given interview by interview. It is about what Mr and Mrs Lorenz could not know of themselves and what they could not hear and understand about each other. The account may at first appear confusing to the reader, just as at times it confused the workers. Like the clients they often did not know, sometimes because Mr and Mrs Lorenz could not let them, sometimes because they also could not hear and understand.

The discussion is in two parts. The second part describes some of the features of the organisation of practice in the Institute which the student-workers found helpful, especially in assisting them to understand and withstand the pressures exerted by disturbed clients.

The first part of the discussion considers the type of pressure the clients put on the two workers; not so much *why*, but *how* Mr and Mrs Lorenz were feeling and not feeling and how this was exhibited in their behaviour together and at the Institute. This description is related to a simple theoretical model of three mental mechanisms, which for the purpose of this paper we shall call "introjection", "projection" and "projective identification". We have excluded discussion on the other mechanisms of defence which they were employing and of other facets of their behaviour in favour of simplification.[3] We believe that many social workers and social work students can be helped in the earlier stages of their professional life by a simpler theoretical model than can be

---

3 For a more comprehensive review of the psychoanalytic knowledge and experience used by the Institute, see, *Marriage: Studies in Emotional Conflict and Growth*. Ed. L. Pincus. Methuen, 1960.

provided by a wider range of ideas concerning interaction between man and man, and between man and his environment. Identification of one aspect of interaction can be more easily assimilated, and thus used in the worker's practice, if sometimes it is allowed in one context to be less confused with other strands in the enormous complexity of human motivation and behaviour, which are as yet a long way from being properly understood in totality. We have definitely simplified; we hope we have clarified.

THE RECORD

The probation officer who referred this case had supervised Mr Lorenz when he came out of borstal; Mr Lorenz had remained in touch with him before and after his marriage.

An application form was sent to Mr and Mrs Lorenz and this was returned two months later. Mr Lorenz, aged thirty, and Mrs Lorenz, aged twenty-four, had been married six years. They had two children, Gerda aged four and John aged three. Mr Lorenz outlined his problem:

> "I easily get into very bad tempers and quite often do and say things which I really do not mean. I am rather afraid of myself for my wife and children."

Mrs Lorenz wrote at very much greater length. Although her husband was basically a good and loving man, he could only show his love by buying presents; he made promises and broke them; he lied and then he lied to cover up the lie; even when everyone knew that he was lying, he would not admit to it; she could not talk to him any more; although he worked hard, he would not pay the bills on time; he needed money to pull out of his pocket to show someone.

In the final paragraph she said:

> "I am a long way from being perfect and perhaps my behaviour goes some way to making him what he is, only he can tell you. His personal hygiene has also a lot to be desired."

The workers wondered what had been happening during this two months. Mr Lorenz had briefly and baldly presented himself as a problem, but did this short statement indicate a language difficulty, or a fear in asking for help? Would he, therefore, find it very difficult to come for interview? Although Mrs Lorenz saw the main difficulties as being of her husband's making, her tentative suggestion that her own behaviour might contribute to his was a first step in being able to use help for herself. It seemed that she would appreciate, although probably with reservation, this small part of her statement being accepted at its face value and not ignored.

Mrs Lorenz

Mrs Lorenz, comfortably plump, did not show signs of strain when she arrived for her interview with Miss B. Her fair hair was taken back and she was simply clothed in a pinafore dress. She spoke easily and, when invited to talk about her difficulties, spoke with little hesitation. She started by talking about her own ill-health. She described the condition of her thyroid, once over-active, then over-reduced, and apparently after eighteen months still not stabilised. She tended to forget what she was doing and was haphazard in her actions. During the previous weekend she had been upset by her husband on two occasions and had felt that she could screw something up in her hands and smash it; tears on her own in the bedroom had partly relieved the tension.

Stressing what a nice and attractive person he was, she then made two major complaints about her husband. The first of these was his continuous lying over very trivial things; it was not the lies that she minded so much as the inconvenience, insecurity and constant need to cover up for him which they caused her. One example she gave was that of the frying pan. He had told a friend, who was a probation officer, that he could get him a very special one at cost price. After several fresh promises and assurances that it was in the store, but not readily to hand, he bought one at retail price and the housekeeping suffered the loss. Several times they had started to buy a house, the raising of the deposit and mortgage was supposedly in hand, but eventually she learned that nothing had been done. The second difficulty was his lack of hygiene. He seldom washed and the smell in the house was often repulsive.

They had had a three-month courtship after she had left her father and stepmother's home. She had had four "mothers", and as she described "my first mother . . . my second mother . . . my third mother . . ." it sounded like a retinue. Her natural mother died when she was three, and Mrs Lorenz had heard people say that her mother was "an especially good person—too good to remain in this life". After her mother's death, she was sent to an aunt in the north of England for a year. When she came back she found her second mother, whom she hated, and who left after another twelve months. Her third mother was a "good person", who shielded her from the wrath of her father, and who remained with him until after Mrs Lórenz's marriage. Her fourth mother had recently been arrested for shoplifting £8 when she had £92 in her handbag. Mrs Lorenz wondered what her father was doing to this woman, as she did not think this sort of crime indicated badness, but rather was a cry for help.

Relations were apparently strained with her father-in-law as well. She said how beastly he had been when he had telephoned and told her that Hans, her husband, had been in prison eight times. She was not going to have people saying that sort of thing about her husband when it was not true. When Miss B. asked her if she was really as unworried about this accusation as she said she was, Mrs Lorenz said that a person's past was their past and had no relation to the present. She did "not want to know." In any case she knew Hans had not been in prison, because as a favour to the probation officer he had appeared on a television programme about borstals, and whereas the ex-prisoners had not shown their faces to the camera, Hans had allowed himself to be seen full face. She presented this information as proof positive, and so convincingly that Miss B., who up to this time had made no comment, began to wonder if she had misread the referral.

Mrs Lorenz continued to talk about her father-in-law and commented on his drinking too much. Although she and Hans liked a drink, they never had more than one or two—they just did "not want to know." Miss B. metaphorically leapt to attention when this phrase was used a second time, and she wondered why Mrs Lorenz did not want to know? Mrs Lorenz looked shocked and uncomprehending and then said she knew perfectly well what were the after-effects of alcohol. She had seen her father-in-law unpleasantly drunk. Miss B. repeated Mrs Lorenz's phrase that she did "not want to know"—at least for herself; she never risked having more than one or two; nor did she want to know for herself about a person's past. Miss B. said she found this surprising, as Mrs Lorenz had shown enormous understanding that her fourth mother had committed an odd and apparently unnecessary crime when she was under stress. She had also told Miss B. that she was under stress from her thyroid condition and the strain from the implications of Hans' lies, rather than the lies themselves, imposed on her. And there were very big implications if a person had been in prison. Why, she repeated, did Mrs Lorenz not want to know? Mrs Lorenz still thought there was nothing she had to know, but her voice was much less certain. She seemed to have understood what Miss B. had said, and without hesitation she decided she would like to come for regular interviews.

When Mrs Lorenz had left, Miss B. went in search of the other worker, Mrs A., and expressed what was by now her inability to know whether Mr Lorenz had been in borstal or not. Together they looked again at the referral which was quite clear. Despite this clarity and despite her own insistence in the interview on taking up Mrs Lorenz's "not-knowing", it seemed that Miss B. had taken over the inability to know. "Has he, or has he not?" she kept on saying. What information would Mr Lorenz disclose in his interview the following day?

Mr Lorenz

Mr Lorenz arrived early. He was a big and burly man, yet looking rather babyish. He rolled and unrolled his newspaper, hitting his knee when he made a point.

He worked as a machine fitter, mainly on assembly work, and as he described this, Mrs A. had visions of his lifting with his large arms the whole factory structure from one site to another. Factories seemed to be tossed round England at an alarming rate.

He had decided to come because he was afraid of his own bad temper and that he might really hurt someone if he did not "do" something now. In an argument at home or at work he often felt he might explode—slap went the newspaper. It had taken him a long time to decide whether to stay away or to come and be "really honest. You see, my trouble is that I am not entirely honest. I do not tell downright lies, but I let people think I mean this or that, and then I say I did not mean that, so they cannot believe me any more." He described the difficult situations this had brought about and he thought his lies were

14

connected with his temper. He did not want to do something "awful" and go back to prison. (Slap)

In view of his own admission that he found it difficult to tell the truth, Mrs A. was relieved to know that he had been able to tell her that he had been in prison. This honesty removed the uncertainty which she in her turn had taken from Miss B. She was then able to ask him what had led up to this, and he told her that he started to get into trouble when he came back to England at the age of thirteen. He had been visiting his grandparents in Austria when the war broke out, and was detained there, with his father, for the duration. He had been placed on probation for offences of stealing and housebreaking and had later been sent to borstal. It was here that he really started to worry about himself. The other boys boasted of their sexual prowess and he thought, "Bloody hell, I've done nothing like that. Am I all right or am I queer?" He remembered that when he was fifteen his father had taken him to a prostitute in Soho and told him to get on with it, but he had turned and run. He married when he was twenty to spite his father. The marriage lasted a week, when he walked out. He did not know what had gone wrong except that she was a girl who did not like men. This was a horrible experience which he had put behind him, as he had the borstal sentences. He did not want his wife, Jean, to know about this, as his past was his past and he now felt he had lived it down.

This seemed to be one long tale of running away from things, and afterwards Mrs A. realised that she could have made some comment about this, but at the time she was only aware that he might very easily run out of the interview. And yet she found she could not put this into words. Despite his size, he made her feel not only motherly, but grossly over-protective, and she wondered why this was so. Was this what he did to his wife? This was in direct contrast to the feeling Miss B. had at the end of her interview with Mrs Lorenz when in astonishment she recalled her Alfred Doolittle-like repetition of, "Why don't you want to know? What don't you want to know?" and had only just restrained herself from adding, "And when will you want to know?" Mrs Lorenz had put into her a toughness which she did not usually feel or express in an initial interview situation.

15

Were Mr Lorenz's ability to make people so protective towards him, and Mrs Lorenz's ability in forcing them to be so persistent, vital factors of their interaction with each other? Consistently overplayed, this would make enormous difficulties for them, but partly explained why he had to go to such lengths in trying to tell her of his criminal record, and why she still could not hear, even when he told an audience of millions through a programme known to be authentic.

Just as Miss B. had become uncertain, so Mrs A. joined in the running away, and did not hear. This secret agreement to play the same game, made consciously or unconsciously, is what we call "collusion". Was this type of collusion also going on in the marriage?

Mrs A. changed the subject and asked him about his experiences in Austria. He could not answer this directly and spoke of his violent likes and dislikes. If he had found that Mrs A. was a German he would have left the room. Still feeling protective Mrs A. nodded approvingly and said nothing. He knew it was not reasonable, he continued, but he could not help it. He had protected his mother, who went to America when he was two, through thick and thin, whatever his father said about her. (Mrs A. felt slightly more comfortable.) Although he had not seen his mother since then, she was still a fact in his life. She was now married and wrote to him, but he could not answer. He longed to know about her and ask her questions, but he could not bring himself to do this. Mrs A.'s nods became even more encouraging, but she could find no words which did not seem too attacking and which might not drive him out.

He then surprised her by saying that he was worried not only that he might be going mad, but that he had no ability to show any feelings. When she *reassured* him that he had shown a great deal of feeling in this interview, he explained that his wife wanted him to cuddle her, but for him sex was all right, "but with me there are no pre-liminaries and no afters, just sex, the same with drink." He would have a couple of beers with the chaps from work, then, getting bored, would leave. He did not even enjoy smoking. When Mrs A. found words and said he seemed to feel there were no lasting pleasures for him, he agreed and thought things went wrong for him as people started by liking him and then changed their minds later. Mrs A. could not run away from these references to herself any longer and finally expressed her understanding of his difficulty; was he wondering whether she might change her mind about him?

When she discussed the question of fees he decided he would be able to manage the money, as his marriage, which he saw as going wrong from the time when Jean started the thyroid trouble and become slapdash, less caring for and more neglectful of himself and the children, was "going down fast" and he wanted "to keep it."

Mr Lorenz recognised his dependence on his wife and saw his security shaken when she became less effective as a housewife and mother, but her ill-health and his lessening control over his temper may have reflected their mutual difficulty in maintaining a continuous charade of a blameless past. He needed her "not-knowing" as a complement to his lies. What was less clear was why she could not know the man she had married. If, despite her affection and the strengths in this marriage, she could not know anything about his past, what could she not know about herself? Had the events or lack of trust in both their lives been too painful to enable them to know a little more honestly the truth about themselves and each other? And was this also reflected in their sexual relationship? Mr Lorenz had suggested he could not know "before or after", and had expressed his doubts about his homosexuality. Consciously or unconsciously, did they share a doubt about their respective sexual identities, and was this all part of what kept them together?

In his first interview Mr Lorenz expressed his fears more clearly than Mrs Lorenz, and placed trust in Mrs A.'s ability to accept the truth about himself, although preparing for the disappointment that she might cease to like him. Mrs A. responded to his enormous effort to come and to tell the truth and wanted to continue to work with him. Miss B. responded similarly to Mrs Lorenz's blatant presentation of being very near "to knowing". In fact both the workers thought there was no decision to make as to whether they did or did not offer them help. They felt they had already started work with this couple and that it would be harmful to turn them away after these interviews, when, with their initial difficulty in coming, they had given so much of themselves.

17

3*

This ability to work and use the interviews was one factor behind the offer of short-term help. It was not assumed that in a period of three months there could be a radical uncovering of truths, but that a slight shift in his ability to tell and in hers to listen, and an easier acceptence that the past could not be deleted as of no consequence in the present, would make the relationship much more comfortable for them both and dispose of the necessity for the more trivial lies over which they were quarrelling. An experience of receiving therapeutic help, even over this short period, might give them a tool with which they could achieve further understanding on their own. They were told, however, that if they wanted to continue for a longer period there would be a change of workers; Mrs A. and Miss B. were leaving the Institute. It was suggested, however, that sometime in the future they might like to come back for another stint. They both accepted the immediate offer for this crisis point in their lives. Mrs A. realised it would not be easy to work with Mr Lorenz, as, despite his determination to speak the truth to her, it was unlikely that he would be able to maintain this, and it would be difficult for her to know when he was lying, or what might seem like a lie to her might be his own particular brand of truth. How much should *she* know?

THE CONTINUATION

Mrs Lorenz

In her second interview Mrs Lorenz presented her worries in a way that made it more difficult for Miss B. to use the material. Mrs Lorenz was concerned for the vendors of the house she and Hans wanted to buy. They were emigrating and wanted the contract signed quickly. Mrs Lorenz was not convinced by Hans' assurances that he could raise the deposit and that his firm would grant a mortgage. When Miss B. took up her own disappointment, rather than that of the vendors, Mrs Lorenz expressed her own doubts whether they could keep up mortgage payments, and she said that what she really wanted was a garden. She talked of the plants which she now grew in the flat, her pride in and success with these. She was steeling herself against the disappointment of not having a garden, although she was as nervous of knowing whether she really could make a beautiful garden, as she had been when she first tried to grow a plant in a pot. The plants were

18

the one thing to which she treated herself out of the house-keeping money which Hans never failed to provide. She carefully justified the rest of her expenditure, but expressed further worry about his not paying the overhead bills until they were threatened with the service being cut off or with eviction. Then he paid. Miss B. felt very frustrated. She did not know what Mrs Lorenz was trying to say to her and the difficulties in buying the house and the care of the plants seemed a long way from knowing whether Mr Lorenz had been in prison or not. Mrs Lorenz seemed to have withdrawn from the last interview when at the end there had seemed to be a close and partially acknowledged understanding.

When Miss B. responded to her difficulty over bills not being paid and her own careful budgeting, Mrs Lorenz then said that they both wanted to go to Austria, where a year ago they had had a very happy holiday. Hans might be able to get a job with an Austrian firm, or they would like to run a hotel there. If they could cut off the past, everything would be all right in Austria. It suited her that she did not know the language, as it enabled her to keep more on the periphery of a group of friends and she did "not have to know" what was going on. She then realised what she had said, and both she and Miss B. laughed.

Miss B. said that although Mrs Lorenz had picked up her own "not knowing", there seemed no magic, like that of moving to Austria, in this interview. Mrs Lorenz then started to talk about the many things that had been stolen from them. Most of these things were her possessions —presents given to her by Hans—which disappeared when they had a lodger in the flat. Hans, who could not bear anyone to be homeless, brought people back to the flat, and then she fed them in such a way and charged such a small sum that they usually stayed for over a year. She described a series of thefts, at first saying that she thought the lodgers must have taken the things, of sentimental rather than monetary value, and later openly admitting that she thought Hans had taken them as a way of getting rid of the lodgers. She did not know why he might want to take back what he had previously given her, although she knew he gave her presents as a way of expressing his affection. If his things disappeared at the same time, they usually turned up later, but this was embarrassing when the insurance had been claimed.

Miss B. still felt rather frustrated and dissatisfied at the end of this interview. It had not had the same momentum as the first. It almost seemed as if she had underheard the importance of Mrs Lorenz's being able to admit, without any direct comment from Miss B., that Hans was stealing her possessions. That she could allow herself to know this was, however, a big step forward for her.

Mr Lorenz

Both Mr and Mrs Lorenz were generous clients; not only were they later able to tell the two workers how things were improving between them, but they also showed in a variety of ways what they had taken back from the interviews and how they were continuing to work out some things between them in the intervals. They had apparently been able to do a little bit more knowing about the past after their first interviews; Mrs Lorenz had found a photograph of Mr Lorenz, then aged twenty-one, in which he had had a beard. He arrived for his interview, again very early, but with three days' growth on his face, and he immediately described his scruffy, dessicated, beatnik appearance at that age. Having told Mrs A. about the finding of the photograph, he continued to talk about his feelings of being different from everyone else; that he did not know where he was born, and therefore he had not been able to get a copy of his birth certificate; of his longing to know his mother, but that knowing what she really felt about him might be worse than not knowing at all. He felt different when he was away from home on a job, and whenever a man used the word "bastard", it nearly "killed him". Mrs A. did not take up the illogicality of the reasons he gave for not being able to obtain a birth certificate, but helped him to explore the feelings about the possibility that he might be illegitimate. He described the humiliation when with six other ex-borstal boys he applied to join the army. He was the only one rejected. He had boasted that he was the lucky one, but he really felt that he was neither English nor Austrian, belonged nowhere, and was no good. He was then able to talk about and to appreciate the difficulty his lies and half-lies made for other people; no one now believed him, even when he spoke the truth; for instance, Jean refused to believe that he had taken a shower at work, when he said he did not want a bath at home. He showed Mrs A. the expensive cookery book he had bought that day to take to Jean. He would like to make a fuss of her, but he could only take her presents.

Mrs Lorenz

Mrs Lorenz's appearance was also changed the next week, so that Miss B. momentarily wondered if she were the same person. She arrived looking almost indecent. She had omitted the blouse from under the pinafore dress, showing a vast expanse of shoulder and bust. Her hair was blonde and her face made up.

She and Hans had decided that it was a great help coming to the Institute, as last week he had gone straight into a bath when he returned from his interview. This was the first bath he had taken without her insistence for years. When he was in the bath he called her, she went in, and they had the first real talk they had ever had, comparing their respective feelings about their mothers.

She was still worried about the house purchase not going through, but was more doubtful whether she really wanted to be tied down with a house in England, when they were both keen on moving to Austria.

At the weekend they had had a row, but she could see how she had driven him out of the house and into the pub. The next morning he had suggested they should all go out in the park together, but she had said she was still in too bad a mood and would spoil the outing. Hans, however, had talked her out of this and said, "Come on, we'll get over it," and apparently they had had a very happy morning. By Sunday evening they were both laughing at their own unreasonableness.

Another child—a motherless one— had been the initial cause of the argument, and when Miss B. helped Mrs Lorenz to wonder why this deprived child had touched off such a lengthy row, she talked more about her own background, the very unhappy year when she returned from the north of England and found a second mother, and a year with another aunt when the second mother had also

21

disappeared. She described herself as a naughty, horrid, little girl, and the aunt would not put up with her. She then went into a children's home at the age of five, but "at least" her father did what he said he would; he had got her out when she was ten and when he had remarried again. But Hans was like her father, in that they both lied to her and let her down.

On this day she talked not so much about the presents Hans had given her as the ones he had forgotten, and the disappointment on her last birthday, which she had felt as a very big let-down. Miss B. asked her what had been the biggest let-down when she was a child. Mrs Lorenz mentioned first a particular present she had wanted from her father, and then that he had promised her her mother's wedding dress. She had never had it and he had given a variety of reasons why he could not find it. She expressed the let-downs in terms of presents, important to both her and Hans as a means of expressing affection, and Miss B. related this to the biggest let-down of all—that her real mother had died.

Mrs Lorenz thought a hard childhood was a good thing, as it made you tough, and then you were not so easily hurt. Miss B. disagreed with this, and thought the hurts were still there underneath, and the presents very important when she had been unsure of her father's love. She then remembered how his presents had arrived every month, but were never what she wanted. She wondered whether alternate generations always over-compensated for what had happened before, as she had made enormous efforts to do well by her children. John was no problem, but she described Gerda as a whiny, demanding child, with whom she became very irritable, giving a very similar picture to that she had given of herself earlier in the interview.

The next week she cancelled her interview because Gerda was ill and she could not leave her.

Mr Lorenz

Mr Lorenz again arrived early for his interview, this time by one hour. He was still unshaven, but generally looked very much smarter. He had forgotten Mrs A.'s name. He talked mainly about his work and how he drove himself to

22

do a good job. This, however, gave him no lasting satisfaction, as it was only making more "filthy lucre for the
bosses." He described situations where he lost his temper
and then people avoided him. Again Mrs A. took this up
in relation to herself, and he then talked about the row at
the weekend. He had suddenly found himself holding a
chair, and without knowing what he was doing, had
splintered the leg. As he described this incident the pers-
piration broke out on his forehead and he visibly trembled
all over. With Mrs A. he was able to look at the way he
expressed his angry feelings in relation to his wife, but not
the loving ones. When he was not angry he was out of
touch, and she felt he neglected her and the children.

Mr Lorenz

The following week the growth on his face was an abundant,
curling beard and he said he had a problem. Work with his
own firm was slack. He had been offered a new job with
£40 a week basic pay, £20 expenses allowances, regardless
of where he went, and a promise of £1,000 worth of equip-
ment. What was the snag? He had not been able to ask
why they had offered him so much. He and Jean had staged
an act and she had pretended to be the interviewing
employer. This had helped him, and they were working
things out better, but he was still the same man and
concerned about this "temper business".

He then exposed many of his deeper fears about himself.
His father had been convicted for causing grievous bodily
harm. Had he inherited this tendency? Was he going
mad? Did his father's temper drive his mother away? He
thought Jean stayed with him only because of the children.
Was he a Jekyll and Hyde? He loved to shock people.
This outpouring of feelings of badness seemed to help him,
but as they were so dissociated from all his strengths,
Mrs A. commented that he seemed to believe that he was
not worth £40 a week. Together they discussed the good
and the bad in himself, particularly in his relationship
with his wife, how he could not know about the goodness
in himself, nor know about the lies and the truth.

As he left he said that his family had all been ladies'
hairdressers, and so had he, but he had then decided to
give it up and do something quite the opposite.

He then did not come for two weeks.

The workers were discussing these interviews week by week, so that each of them knew what had happened in the other interviews. As their knowledge of the work is now retrospective and tempered by hindsight, and the discussions, some optimistic, some depressed and lethargic, were not recorded, it is difficult to reproduce accurately the ideas and suggestions they made at the time in answer to each other's queries in an attempt to understand what was happening. What can be remembered, however, is some of the feelings. There were underlying feelings of anxiety and inadequacy, and envy of the other worker when their own client failed to come for an interview (always harder to tolerate when the workers are students and wanting to prove themselves, or even compete with the other students as to their respective ability to be helpful). There were the feelings of motherliness which Mrs A. continually expressed in relation to Mr Lorenz— "he made me feel so protective;" and the feelings of toughness, which Miss B. still felt when she had done some work in an interview with Mrs Lorenz, or of ineffectualness, when she had been unable to use the material Mrs Lorenz presented. They were even surer that these feelings put into their partnership were indicative of what was going on in Mr and Mrs Lorenz's marriage.

The reader's questions are no doubt the same as those Mrs A. and Miss B. asked each other. Why was Mr Lorenz becoming increasingly anxious about his interviews, arriving earlier and earlier each time? What was it that propelled him to the Institute, and then why did he fail to appear for two weeks after what had been a very moving interview for both him and Mrs A.?

How had he interpreted to himself over the years the loss of his mother? He stood up for her "through thick and thin", but he felt really in touch with his wife only when he was angry. Why, despite his efforts, did he have to be so punishing to her, even when she was so important to him?

And why, asked Miss B., taking over the part of her client, did Mrs Lorenz put up with this? What did her father mean to her? He had been the most stable figure in her childhood, even if not a very satisfactory one. Had she tried to identify with him? Underneath her anger against him for having so many replacement wives, for bringing her the wrong presents, for leaving her in a children's Home, how much did she love and want to be like him, and how much did she want his love in return? Was this old conflict of jealousy and mixed love and anger what she was trying to solve with the man she chose to marry? Was Hans enough like her father to give her a *second chance,* and yet different enough to give her more chance of succeeding? If she succeeded with Hans, would she put at rest some of the old unhappiness of her childhood, in which something had happened —something about "not knowing"– which still prevented her knowing in the present situation with a man, who not only demanded her protection and a situation of not knowing, but also told more than enough lies for two of them?

These interviews had opened some channels of communication previously closed between this couple. But what was the connection between being clean and being able to talk about mothers? Now a little bit cleaner and smarter, was Mr Lorenz a little bit less depressed?

Interrupting again, Miss B. wondered not so much whether Gerda's ailment had really necessitated her staying away from school, but why Mrs Lorenz, who used a baby-sitter on other occasions, chose to miss an interview after one which ended by her talking about this child in similar terms to herself?

What did her radically changed and provocative appearance mean? Sex had not been mentioned in her interviews, but was this an indication that she was now nearer to exposing this part of herself? Or was the greater exposure of her flesh a bodily representation of what she felt the interviews were doing to her? Or was this how she dressed and looked before she met Hans, just as he was re-growing the beard he had sported when he was twenty-one?

Mrs Lorenz

After her week away looking after Gerda, her appearance changed again. The blonde hair and the bare flesh had disappeared. She personified a demure mother in suitable, careful clothes that would not show the dirt, and her appearance was made even more drab by the addition of thick, black stockings. (It was midsummer.) She had nothing to talk about. Hans had been away on a new job. Nothing had happened.

Soon, however, she recaptured her fairly fluent way of speaking, and said that they both wondered whether the money was "too good to be true." While he was away she had been able to get on doing things on her own, and had been learning German. She could not do this when he was at home, as, although he had suggested she bought the linguaphone records, he could not stand the noise when she played them. She talked of their difficulties in sharing activities and jobs and of her resentment that women "do all the work." She described her thyroid condition as worse, even more unstabilised, so that some days she was very over-active, some days very limp. On the days she came for the interviews she was at her most forgetful, had to get off the bus because she had forgotten her purse, and could not think of anything she wanted to talk about.

Mrs Lorenz

The following week she was feeling worse and had been to the hospital again about her thyroid. She had been told that they had corrected the deficiency, but had not found the underlying cause. She had felt so unwell that morning that she had not wanted to come for this interview.

Miss B. could not ignore this a second time, and, having discussed the last interview with her supervisor, she now related the feeling unwell and Mrs Lorenz's difficulty in coming to the Institute with her feelings for Miss B. Miss B. suspected that these were very mixed; although Mrs Lorenz found when she arrived that she could talk about the difficulties in the marriage, and had said that some things were a little better between her and Hans, the interviews were hard and painful work. Miss B. was very conscious of this, not only for Mrs Lorenz but for herself; she thought Mrs Lorenz must resent her for the part she played in this, making her work and making her look at herself. She thought that Mrs Lorenz's mixed feelings of wanting to come and not wanting to come were probably very similar to the mixed feelings she had for her mother—love and yet at the same time resentment that she had died and left her. Miss B. was very conscious that it would have helped Mrs Lorenz if she had acknowledged this difficulty in coming the previous week, when there had been the first reference to her not being so well. Because she herself was not sure which of the two—disappearing mother figures, or a father who had lost or who had driven out three women—were of the greater emotional significance to Mrs Lorenz in her

26

present relationships, she now left no stone unturned; as an afterthought to her explanatory remark, she suggested that Mrs Lorenz's feelings for Miss B. were probably as mixed as her feelings about her father.

Mrs Lorenz apparently ignored this, but it seemed to have meaning for her, as later in the interview she herself made a connection between her own behaviour and that of her father. But at the time, perhaps because the relationship between herself and Miss B. had been better clarified, she changed the subject to what concerned her most, and as in the previous interview she started to talk again about the difficulties she and Hans had in sharing—there was always a clash as to who was to be foreman.

Like many types of jobs, social work is often very repetitive. One can speculate now whether Mrs Lorenz's having missed one interview slowed down the pace of the work. Was she telling Miss B. very firmly "not so fast"? Or had Miss B. not heard well enough—was she the one who was slack, the one who had an off-day? But, whether Mrs Lorenz had previously been testing out Miss B. and had been biding her time at her own pace or not, she, like most clients, repeated the theme. This time, however, she took it a little further and expressed it not so much in terms of her resentment, but in a recognition of her own needs. Taking over Miss B.'s language, she explained that she wanted more support and fathering from Hans, whereas he wanted her to be mother and father in one, not giving anything back. Perhaps because she felt they had both underworked the previous week, perhaps because she felt guilty that she had not supported Mrs Lorenz enough, perhaps because she was answering this direct cry to be allowed to be childlike, Miss B. now supported Mrs Lorenz's new insight into her own needs, and said that, as for most people, these needs were legitimate; that it was only when the "child" took over inappropriately or unproductively, or was in too much conflict with the other person's "child", that the "adults" suffered and the sharing became so difficult.

Another difficulty in the marriage, Mrs Lorenz said, was intercourse. She did not enjoy it and even hated being kissed. Although she had heard her friends talk about their sexual practices, and really knew they were neither indecent nor unnatural, in relation to herself she did not like the ideas. She immediately switched to Hans and quickly said that she thought the main difficulty was that he smelt; he had not bathed at all during the last weekend. But after a pause, during which Miss B. did not say anything, but in which her disbelief of this may have been felt, Mrs Lorenz wondered if her own lack of feeling in bed might be to do with her father. Miss B. asked her what she meant by this and she explained it in terms of his having had so many women one after the other. Together they wondered what this meant to her as a young child, particularly as her father had "carried on" with his second wife before her own mother died. Miss B. then said that although Mrs Lorenz had now gone a long way in realising that some of the difficulty in bed lay in her own mixed-up feelings, she thought Hans' smelling had been very useful to Mrs Lorenz over the years in providing a good reason for her distaste; this had enabled her to keep her own difficulty out of sight.

Although at the time this remark seemed appropriate and well-held in a relationship which by now was strong enough to take this type of truth, in retrospect it seemed to Miss B. to have been too much of a broadside. Mrs Lorenz had acknowledged it with a look which was similar to the one she had given Miss B. in the first interview after she had said, "Why don't you want to know?"

Mrs Lorenz

Not surprisingly, perhaps, Mrs Lorenz arrived early for her next interview. Previously she had always been ten minutes late. She seemed very anxious and, before she sat down, she told Miss B. that the hospital doctor said her thyroid condition affected her sexual desire. She did not actually say, "So there," but Miss B. could hear it reverberating round the four walls like a ball in a squash court. Miss B.'s own anxiety seemed justified. But as Mrs Lorenz sat down, she sighed, and said she also wanted to tell Miss B. that she had been right about the usefulness of Hans' smelling. Last weekend he had had a bath, was very clean and fresh and wanted intercourse. She was niggly and horrid to him, and now realised it

28

was her, not him. She also knew the interviews affected her health. She was always worse on the morning she came, and that morning she could hardly get out of bed. But she was much better during the rest of the week. Miss B. relaxed, and let out a different sort of inaudible sigh—one of relief.

The new job was not working out; the firm was making such a tight schedule for Hans that he would not be able to get home for the weekends. Although for a few weeks it had helped them to be separated for a few days, they now knew they needed each other and could not stand eight weeks apart.

In their discussion Mrs A. and Miss B. had wondered how much Mr Lorenz's changing his job had been connected with the work at the Institute. Often when couples are re-sorting out their relationship there needs to be a time of temporary separation. The new job had for a time served this well. They were now, however, reaffirming their need of each other, but Mrs Lorenz went on to express her doubts as to their ability to handle the togetherness better. The house purchase, she said, was still over their heads, but much as she wanted a home and garden of her own, she was scared whether they could manage. She talked a lot about her plants, how she was able to grow indoor ones with which other people failed, but at first it had taken her two years to have the courage to try. She related this to her father who had been a keen and good gardener, and her never being allowed to help him. Miss B. felt very aware of Mrs Lorenz's initial deprivation, and the temporary pain she herself caused her when she made comments which would increase Mrs Lorenz's understanding of some of her feelings. But her awareness of Mrs Lorenz's strength with which she had attempted to overcome her feeling of insecurity, enabled her to take Mrs Lorenz's suggestion a little further. She said she thought Mrs Lorenz had not been able to let herself be like her father, either as a gardener, or as a person with sexual desire, and that Hans' not settling the mortgage served her doubts about taking on a house and garden, as his smelling had served her sexual difficulty. Yes, Mrs Lorenz thought; perhaps this was true as well.

She continued to talk of her difficulty in dealing with Hans' lies. She was now always wanting proof that what he said was true. Miss B. asked her what else in her life had needed proof—could she remember any big lie which had been told to her as a child? This was a "professional guess", which enabled Mrs Lorenz to mention one of the most significant facts in her history. This went a long way to explain why she could not allow herself "to know" The information came, however, only in the sixth interview. There was a long pause after Miss B.'s question, and then Mrs Lorenz said that she had never been told that her mother had died. When she came back from the north and found her second mother, her father told her that her mother had been in hospital a year and had merely changed her name. But Mrs Lorenz remembered her father coming back from the funeral. When she was nine she heard a remark which made her again query the identity of her second mother and she asked her grandmother who then told her of her mother's death. With Miss B. she talked of the awfulness of this, and, as Miss B. put it, which was the worse to know—that her mother had died, or had changed into this person she hated, who later deserted. No wonder she found it difficult to know.

From this Mrs Lorenz went on to talk about her forgetfulness, and of the type of things she forgot which surprised her. During the week she forgot these interviews and only remembered what had been said the day before coming to the next one. Although she made an effort to keep the house clean and tidy, she always forgot to make her and Hans' bed. Miss B. said that forgetting was a way of dealing with ideas that were too difficult to hold and tolerate, and perhaps she could remember the interviews only when she was about to come back, knowing she and Miss B. could hold these ideas together. Her feelings about sex being distasteful and dirty, and the bedroom forgotten and left dirty, were also connected and were something to do with her distaste that her father had had too many women.

Mrs Lorenz said that she and Hans had big disagreements about the clothes she wore. She did not like flashy, bright colours, as she thought she might be picked up in the street. But Hans wanted her to wear a mini skirt. Again

Miss B. put this back to Mrs Lorenz that she feared, if she made herself attractive to Hans, he would want more sex, and that if she allowed herself more, she might take too much. If she allowed herself an inch, would she take a yard, and have too many men as her father had had too many women?

Mr Lorenz

Miss B. felt she had been, if not over-active in the interview with Mrs Lorenz, at least very persistent. This was in contrast to Mrs A. who sat in solitary state for an hour the next day when Mr Lorenz did not arrive at the Institute for his interview. She left the Institute when the hour was up and met him between the building and the tube station. He looked like a small child caught in the act of doing something wrong and seemed to be waiting for her. She had to make a split-second decision whether to go along with this bit of testing her out, delaying her own return home, or whether to be firm as the interview time was now over. She decided that if he wanted to be caught, she would catch him, and when he smiled anxiously at her, she greeted him, offered him an alternative interview there and then, and they returned to the Institute.

There he said he was very muddled. He had left his job and was now doing casual work while he tried to find what he really wanted—work satisfaction and wonderful pay. Mrs A. thought this referred to what was going on between him and her, the lack of satisfaction that everything was not solved and the shortage of time in which they still had to work. Mr Lorenz explained his difficulty in that he could either become so attached to Mrs A. that it would be unbearable to come, or he could hate her. As this was so obviously related to his feelings for his mother, he and Mrs A. talked about her again, and Mr Lorenz said he wished he could untell the lie he had told his wife, that he had met his mother. Then he started to talk about the sexual relationship with his wife. Because he was part Austrian, people expected him to be passionate, but really he thought he was a cold man who needed only infrequent sex. As he talked about this it became more clearly part of his inablilty to let himself get close to people. He wished he could share his work problems with Jean, but she saw his work only in

31

terms of wages. He could not tell her that it was his feelings and his muddle that he wanted her to understand. He thought some of the things talked out in the interview got lost and never said to his wife; Mrs A. suggested that they might like to consider having a joint interview.

The following week he missed his appointment, but Mrs Lorenz reported that things were very much better.

Mrs Lorenz

Although Hans was so tired when he got back at the weekend, he had later emerged from his bed and taken them all out. They had had a marvellous time.

She had found that she had regained her powers of concentration and had been learning German very quickly. Hans had helped her with the pronunciation and had said what better place to do it than in the bath.

He had changed his underwear every day. She could hardly keep up with the washing.

He had paid off some of the outstanding bills and given her more housekeeping money.

He had been extremely kind and helped her to talk about her difficulty in not wanting sex. She had told him that she had discovered it was her fault. Although he had been so patient and helpful in bed, she was upset to find that she was still unmoved.

She had also discovered that she could let Hans go. Previously she felt when he went away that only half of her existed.

The one difficulty which had marred the week was over the bottle garden. When she said she wanted one, Hans had gone out and bought one for her. He had helped put in the earth and then had wanted to buy the plants and plant them. Mrs Lorenz could not allow this, and could not visualise what plants she wanted. She described herself as being uncreative and needing to get ideas from other bottle gardens on display in the shops. When Miss B. discussed with her this difficulty in sharing and the need for the bottle garden to be perfect, rather than their own joint and imperfect effort, she described other difficulties in sharing and making compromises; at one point she made a slip of the tongue, saying "I'm always right," correcting

32

herself quickly to, "I'm always wrong." Miss B. would not accept the correction and related this slip to her previous difficulty of being right or wrong as to whether her mother was dead or not, and whether she thought Miss B. was right or wrong.

In this interview Mrs Lorenz expressed her awareness of the shortage of time before the work finished. She had taken her driving test that week, and knew she had taken it too soon, really needing very much more practice. Miss B. expressed her understanding of this reference, and, acknowledging the improvements in the marriage, said she understood the feeling of panic that Mrs Lorenz felt—that Miss B. was asking too much of her in too short a time. They were both very aware there were only a few weeks left.

Mrs Lorenz

The next week Mrs Lorenz described how she had been able to let Hans plant the bottle garden for her. She had had to cover her eyes, saying, "Don't be so rough, you'll damage them," but, despite his handling, the plants were all thriving well and truly. He had been searching the shops for a special plant she wanted to climb round the structure in the middle.

On one evening Hans had said that he felt sexy, and then she had provoked a row. She was not aware at the time that she had done this, but later in the evening Hans had pointed this out, and they agreed they would not have had this row if he had not made the overture.

Much of this interview was about Gerda's behaviour and Mrs Lorenz's feelings about her and John. Father's Day had been a great disappointment when Hans failed to acknowledge suitably the card, with a picture of an Austrian lake, which the children had given him. In talking about Hans, however, she showed very much more compassion for him than previously, and decided that in the long run it was easier for her that her mother had died than for him not knowing why his mother had deserted him. Hans had now talked to her about what it had been like living in Austria during the war.

But still she did not know whether he had been in prison or not. She wondered about this, and Miss B. suggested a joint interview, which Mrs Lorenz thought might be useful.

It had taken eight interviews for Mrs Lorenz to be able to come back to the crucial question as to whether she could know if her husband had been in prison or not. She seemed only able to do this after the reason for her difficulty in knowing what was right and what was wrong had been clarified a little, and after she and Hans had re-tested out their ability to share with each other. The fact that, despite his (and Miss B.'s) rough handling, the plants still lived, must have given her a great deal of reassurance as to the strength in the marriage.

Both Mrs A. and Miss B. thought a joint interview might be needed during the course of the work, but were unsure when it should be timed within this brief span. Some of Mr and Mrs Lorenz's difficulties had seemed to need single interviews for their expression, before they could share them together; but they had now both given an opening which allowed the workers to suggest a joint interview. When Mr Lorenz then missed an interview the workers wondered if the suggested date was too soon and did not allow enough time for them to get used to the idea; quite apart from the fact that he had had one interview less on his own before the joint one, was his staying away something to do with a fear that he would lose Mrs A. in the bigger group? Would he feel under attack in an interview with three women, when many of his basic difficulties in relating to the female sex were still a long way from being resolved? Although Mrs A. knew from Miss B. (and knew that Mr Lorenz would know she knew) that things were very much better, Mr Lorenz was not able, in the same way as his wife, to show his own worker his affection and charity, nor tell her of the changes that were taking place. The two workers wondered if the joint interview should be put off a week, but they agreed that if they put it off any longer there would not be enough time afterwards to work through any repercussions that might arise.

Mr Lorenz

At his interview Mr Lorenz did express directly his worry at the prospect of this joint interview. He wondered if he would take an instant dislike to Miss B., and, "if I do—and I've got my defences too—I won't speak to her at all." Mrs A. accepted this plea and reassured him that if he wanted a single interview instead, the arrangement could be changed.

34

He talked of his difficulty in keeping contact with people. He was delighted that he had received a birthday card from his mother. He wondered if he could now write to her, but he had no picture of her. When Mrs A. asked him if this was what it was like when he could not telephone her himself to alter an interview—had he no picture of her when he was not actually at the interview—he replied he could not telephone America, because he could not say in three minutes what would take an hour. Mrs A. thought this was the parallel statement to Mrs Lorenz's having said she had taken her driving test too early; like her he was very aware of the shortage of time; the end of this piece of work was coming too soon.

In this interview he was very muddled and concerned because he had turned down a good job. He wanted to take it, but it carried more responsibility and he did not think he was good enough for it. He might get into more tempers and blow everything "sky high". Sometimes he felt he could kill someone. When Mrs A., who by this time was becoming aware that he could not express directly his anger against her, but was splitting this off on to Miss B. whom he was preparing to dislike, suggested that this someone was his mother for having deserted him, he told of his shame about his bad behaviour on Father's Day. It was too much when Jean and the children woke him up and confronted him with a card depicting an Austrian scene. He did not want to think about Austria, he said, and he described a twilight state when he could not wake up and respond to their gesture. His childish feelings and outburst of temper made it all seem a ghastly failure.

The following day he telephoned when Mrs A. was not at the Institute and spoke to Miss B. He cancelled the joint interview on the arranged day, and then asked for another date. This telephone call seemed very important to him particularly as he talked to Miss B.; he prepared himself a little more for meeting her. Mrs A. thought he had done this on purpose and had to make an initial contact with the "unseen mother", who could be the bad one, whereas he could not telephone his own worker whom he had to keep good.

The Joint Interview

Mrs A. and Miss B. were hopeful and excited at the prospect of the joint interview, believing that Mr Lorenz would be able to tell his wife that he had been in prison, and that she might ease the telling for him and be able to listen. In the event their hopes were naive and premature, and the main value of the very flat interview was that Mr and Mrs Lorenz were able to come together and share their workers. Mr Lorenz took the initiative and told Mrs A., with surreptitious glances at Miss B., that he had been offered and had accepted a job in Austria at £3,000 a year. They had been having long discussions recently and had sorted out many things. They saw the move to Austria as a new start to their marriage. Mrs Lorenz thought the marriage up till now had been on her terms. In Austria she would be the weaker partner, and he would have to take more responsibility. She would not be able to get involved in his business on the telephone. It would all be up to Hans. He thought he was capable of this, and both of them thought they would have more family and more support in Austria. Hans had an understanding godmother there, of whom he was very fond, and he wanted to share her with Jean. They would also have to share the "bad", difficult grandmother. Hans thought he would feel more at home in Austria, and that he would be able to get in touch with the earlier part of his life.

They presented themselves very much as a married couple keeping at bay the two workers who listened to their plans, but were quite unable to do anything useful with the material they presented. Although Mr Lorenz did not actively show a dislike for Miss B., his reference to the "good godmother" and the "bad grandmother" suggested he had to split off his likes and dislikes very firmly, but was attempting to share them and his good worker with his wife. Miss B. was very aware in this interview of the enormous pressure Mr Lorenz put on people to protect him, and joined with Mrs A. in reassuring him and in filling the silences when he and Mrs Lorenz were not sure how to use the time. Both the workers stressed that Mr and Mrs Lorenz would not be leaving two people behind, but would be taking themselves, their strengths and their weaknesses with them. Mr and Mrs Lorenz seemed to be able to recognise this, but were adamant that the more clearly defined roles of men and women in Austria would be of help to them.

36

Mrs Lorenz

The next week in her single interview Mrs Lorenz reported that the plans for Austria were going ahead. Hans had already started work with the firm, and they would travel the following week. The whole family would go over with Hans for a preliminary period to see how it worked out, before disposing of the flat in England. She thought Hans seemed very much happier working with Austrians. She described the type of job and an incident which to Miss B., not knowing much about the morals in industry, sounded very much like a piece of industrial espionage. At least Mrs Lorenz was now recognising and could know about his delinquency. She then talked of now wanting to be more herself. She thought that in the past she had lived in and through Hans, despite his difficulties. When he had been away working, she had not been able to leave the house. Although her thyroid still seemed to be very unstable, it did not incapacitate her now. She talked of her new energy, the spring cleaning she had done, the mending, the washing and the packing she had done for Austria. Everything was so much easier between her and Hans. She went over their plans, showing some realistic concern for the difficulties there might be and how much she would *choose to know* about his business.

She also wanted to tell Miss B. that she had gone to visit an aunt and talked with her about what really happened when she was a child and found her second mother. The aunt had told her that she had screamed for three days, shrieking that this woman was not her mother. She had then given in, and again Miss B. emphasised the awfulness of not knowing whether the truth was worse than the untruth.

Mrs Lorenz cancelled her husband's interview for the following day. This was contrary to her usual practice of telephoning Mrs A. direct. Miss B. never gave this message another thought and forgot to pass it on to Mrs A. When she learnt that Mrs A. had waited the hour for Mr Lorenz, she felt very abashed, and ruefully they both realised how successfully Mr Lorenz had succeeded in splitting them off into the good who waited and the bad who did not tell. Miss B. had even acted this out for him and had gone along with an attempt to exclude Mrs A. not only from the work, but from knowing about the work, when these might have been the last two interviews. They wondered whether this was his final rejection of Mrs A., if he had felt let down by not having her to himself in the joint interview, or whether he would be able to come back before leaving for Austria.

Neither of the two workers doubted the validity of the move to Austria or the salary. Mrs Lorenz had made a provisional arrangement for the following week, depending on the exact date of the move.

Mrs Lorenz

She did come for this interview and was very concerned and upset about Hans' lying. First she described an incident when she knew he had been lying on the telephone about a private business deal. She was also concerned whether "going to Austria" was another big lie. She wondered if the job really existed, or if it did, what it really entailed. The date for leaving had been altered three times, and she had finally become suspicious when Hans suggested they took a boat out on the river for the weekend, three days after the latest travelling date. She wondered whether he dared to tell her the job had fallen through.

This was the penultimate interview. When Miss B. suggested that Mrs Lorenz must be very angry that, after all this work, she and Mrs A. were still leaving them with their original problem, Mrs Lorenz started to wonder whether Hans had been in prison or not. Having previously appeared to be nearer to being able to know, she now expressed great doubts whether she wanted to know; she could not anticipate what she would feel if it turned out that he had been. She used to think that a person's past did not matter, but now she knew it did affect them, and she wondered if she would be prejudiced.

It was a dispirited pair of workers who discussed this interview. The work and the Lorenzs seemed to be back at square one. Mrs Lorenz's anxiety that Austria was "one big lie" took over, and they really felt that they had been taken for a very long ride. And there might be no more interviews.

Mr Lorenz

Mr Lorenz came the next day, however, and he arrived half an hour early for his appointment, looking very spruce, shaven and in a clean white shirt. He started the interview by discussing in a much more mature way the proposed move to Austria, and it soon became clear that he was very worried by the new "Hans" he expected himself to be in that country. He did not think he could achieve this, yet he did not know what to do. There was a great deal of indecision as to when he should travel; he described a situation in which he had three bosses, one Austrian, one English and one American; and here he became quite lyrical; one boss said he was to leave, another said not, and the third said he did not know. His bosses, like his feelings, seemed split up between three countries. Mrs A. wondered again whether the new job and the proposed move were sheer fantasy.

He then became very upset and said he had had to come to this interview, as he knew he had to tell Jean about his past, but he was terrified of doing this, as she then might leave him. But it was now intolerable for them to go on without his telling her. He was adamant that he could not tell her himself; he had tried many times and failed; he wanted a mediator, a person or a machine who would do this. He thought Mrs A. was rather like a machine; he could tell anything to her; she heard all and she "still went on"; he could even tell her that he was queer, and this would make no difference. Mrs A. sat, trying not to flinch— a machine, who did not care about anything. How she must have failed him, she thought. Steadily losing confidence, she wondered if she really had behaved like a machine; she felt useless when he said, "You don't have to know about the feelings", and she momentarily forgot the outpouring of feeling for which he had used her previously. But he cared for Jean, he went on to say, and that was why he could not tell her; his marriage was the most important thing to him. He asked Mrs A. if she would be the mediator; he would feed the information to her, and she must pass it on to his wife. When Mrs A. explained that the facts were only part of the situation, and that the telling, the sharing and the knowing was the bigger part and the important experience for them both, he protested that he still could not do it. Eventually, when Mrs. A had given him extra time, he thought he could tell Jean that he had a great deal on his mind which he found difficult to tell, and he would then see what happened.

The next day Mrs Lorenz telephoned and asked to speak to Mrs A. Hans had told her he had something to tell, but had been unable to go any further; he wanted Mrs A. to do the telling. Mrs A. spoke to her first, saying she could not do this, and then Miss B. spoke to her and tried to help her feel safer in helping Hans to tell, and in her being able to listen. It was arranged that if he were not able to tell her over the weekend, he might like to come to her interview at the beginning of the following week.

On the Monday Mrs Lorenz telephoned again. It had been an "awful" weekend, and they had not been able to discuss anything. A joint interview was arranged for the first half hour of the appointment, to be followed by two single interviews for the remainder of the time.

The Second Joint Interview

Mr Lorenz arrived early, Mrs Lorenz late. Mr Lorenz could not look at anyone, and sat anxiously on the edge of the chair wringing his hands. He said he had been under a misapprehension and understood that he could see Mrs A. on his own and then leave. When it became clear that this was being built into a big crisis situation, and that he would not be able to tell, the workers should probably have terminated the joint interview and continued with single ones. But, believing that he might have to leave the telling until the last few minutes, they re-stated the time allowed for the joint interview. With his head in his hands Mr Lorenz told them there was not one thing he had to tell, but six. (Murder—arson—rape—treason—manslaughter—forgery, flashed through the minds of the workers.) He expressed all his anger against Miss B., who was the one he could not tell. Repeatedly he said he could tell only Mrs A.; then he would like to leave so that she could pass on the information to Jean. Mrs Lorenz said that now things had come to a point when she had to know. If he could not tell her, she could not bear this strain any longer, and this would break the marriage. Both Mrs A. and Miss B. made several interpretations as to why it was difficult for him to tell, and for her to hear, but these were ineffective. Just before the time was up, Mrs Lorenz made what was an innocuous remark in a most provocative way, and Mr Lorenz, saying, "You just don't understand," bolted through the door.

40

Mrs Lorenz and Miss B. continued with a single interview, while Mrs A. waited in case Mr Lorenz was able to return, but there was no further sign of him.

Miss B. told Mrs Lorenz that she thought she and Hans had had to show the two workers the difficulties they still had in front of them, before they left the Institute, and that this crisis was connected with the withdrawal of her and Mrs A.'s support. Mrs Lorenz said that ten weeks previously she would have gone along with the lies, but now she felt more under a strain because she had to know. She felt inadequate in her ability to help him to tell. Miss B. encouraged her to voice her fantasies as to what Hans could have done—what to her would be the worst. Mrs Lorenz did not think she could bear it if he had assaulted a child.

At the end of this last interview the two workers thought they had failed in one of the main objectives of the work. They questioned why they had failed, they wondered what they had not understood and they searched for a reason as to why they had not been able to help him to tell and her to listen. All theory disappeared in one big and united despair. They could barely see how manipulative Mr Lorenz had been, although several times during the joint interview they had felt like puppets on a string. They realised how angry he had been, particularly with Mrs A., even though this was expressed against Miss B.; only tentatively did they consider the supervisor's suggestion that his building up the telling situation into such a big crisis was only another indication of his exaggerated responses—this time to the loss of the workers. They had laughed at the factories being tossed round England, but not when they were the objects whom he attempted to toss. It was suggested that the crisis had to be acted out at the Institute to prevent a bigger one being prolonged in the home; but, as they themselves were departing, they did not like leaving the case in the middle of a crisis. They were not sure whether their insistence on refusing to take the responsibility for the telling had been maintained long enough to be a meaningful learning experience for Mr and Mrs Lorenz. After only twelve weeks of work could Mr and Mrs Lorenz now resolve this on their own? They were sure they had been right in their refusal to deprive Mr and Mrs Lorenz of the shared experience of telling and listening, but, going round in circles, they wondered painfully how they could have better helped them to achieve this for themselves.

41

The next morning Mrs Lorenz telephoned Miss B. Hans had told her—or at least he had written it down and immediately left the house. It was all right, not nearly as bad as she had expected, and when she read it, she sat down and laughed. He had been in prison three times, he had lived with a prostitute, he had never seen his mother, and he had never been in the army. She was worried how long he would stay out of the house, and how she could help him when he came back. They were leaving for Austria in two days, and neither of them wanted to see the workers again.

She thought they could now manage on their own.

The two workers also felt better able to manage leaving the Institute the following day.

DISCUSSION

The first part of this discussion considers not why Mr and Mrs Lorenz had to behave in the way that they did, but how they were behaving together, and how they were feeling and not feeling.

Mr Lorenz's feelings were so intense that he could not put them on to paper, took two months to come for an interview, and then confessed to great fear of madness. He expressed the extremes. If he allowed himself to love the helpful Mrs A. it would be unbearable; and perhaps we might add, particularly when she eventually deserted him. He expressed his feelings not only in ungrammatical but always vivid English, but also, like a child, in many of his bodily poses and gestures. Outside the interviews, he seemed to be able to get himself into, and to help to create, situations and crises, which portrayed these very confused feelings for him, and which may have offered him release from the tension which they caused him. His amount of bad feeling seemed very disproportionate to his present circumstances, in which he had a good work record, a loving wife and two healthy children.

Mrs Lorenz had also suffered an enormous loss in her childhood, and had been subjected too often to change and insecurity; she was still suffering from the unfortunate consequences of the crises and situations into which her husband's feelings propelled them. But she thought a hard childhood made a person tough, and, when Hans failed to do anything about getting a mortgage, she was concerned only for the vendors who would be so disappointed. Apparently she did not have any feelings of great loss, or pain, or even of disappointment. But one of the attributes of humanity is a capacity for feeling, and in other respects she did not show herself to be a robot or without this capacity; she seemed very human; she loved her husband and her children and much of her care of them exemplified this. She could feel some feelings, but not others which were appropriate to the circumstances. They seemed to have been split off. But what had happened to them?

43

Mrs Lorenz was not showing enough feeling of sorrow and hurt, but Mr Lorenz was showing a disproportionate amount, particularly of angry feelings, which shut out his more loving ones. They were so strong that he continually tried to run away from them, into prison, out of a first marriage after only a week, and through a pattern of behaviour of trivial and unnecessary lies and outbursts of temper which muddled and angered people and terminated the relationships. Although in this marriage there seemed to be a misassortment of feelings, with too many on one side and not enough on the other, Mr and Mrs Lorenz wanted to stay together and seemed to know that they could not do without each other. He needed her to be feelingless and to be the strong one while his feelings were so muddled and his actions so erratic, and she needed him to express for her the feelings she could not feel. She seemed to be consistent in this behaviour pattern of not being able to know her own feelings; even on social occasions she could not know for herself what it was like to get a little drunk; during and at the end of the second interview it was Miss B. who was made to feel frustrated and ineffectual, although looking back there was a slight shift in Mrs Lorenz's ability to know, which was appropriate to what was only the second meeting. When Miss B. did try to push some feeling back into Mrs Lorenz and refused to believe her lack of disappointment about the house purchase, Mrs Lorenz could at first only express feelings of doubt about keeping up payments, and then only tentatively express her disappointment about a garden. While Mrs Lorenz still could not allow herself to feel her own disappointment and her own frustration that there was no easy magic or way of change, Miss B. seemed to carry an unjustified amount. She was the one who was disappointed and frustrated and inappropriately muddled about the "irrelevance" of the material, which only later with her supervisor could she see as very relevant.

We do not know how people manage to put feelings (which are either appropriate or inappropriate to the situation in which they find, or manage to find, themselves) out of their own psychological system into that of another person. We do know, however, from direct observation, that people can do this and unknowingly have to do this when the feelings are too painful and too highly charged for them to be able to hold on to them in their own mind. It appears that when they need to get rid of the feeling completely they are able to dispose of it into another person (or into a personified institution) whom they then keep out of sight if not out of mind. There is then less possibility of their being forced by the recipient to take it back into themselves, or of their knowing that the supposed recipient does not accept it.

In this paper we are calling the mechanism of putting feelings outside the owner and into another person, "projection"[4]. Often, when people talk vehemently about another person, expressing gross intolerance of that person's behaviour, they are in effect saying that they cannot acknowledge in their own selves the primitive feelings, which may well underlie that type of behaviour, but which are also part of their own human ancestry. If these particular feelings are allowed to remain as part of their own conscious being, they might be translated into action similar to that of the person they criticise; it is safer to dispose of them completely.

When, however, people are not so adept at splitting off the feeling in this way, and in the inherent growth process are psychologically trying to repair the split and bring the feeling back into themselves, so that they can feel more whole and integrated, they choose an adjacent person, with whom they can continue an ongoing and live relationship, to be their recipient. If this person belongs to them, as in our culture a spouse is seen to belong to his partner, or as a child is seen to belong to his parent, they are still owning this output bit of themselves, and there is the anticipation that if the other person is able to master the feeling, this is then achieved for them too. This process we call, "projective identification"[5], and it can occur only when the recipient tacitly and often unknowingly agrees to accept a feeling to which he is already accustomed and which he knows for himself in his own experience. The acceptance of a feeling from another person we call "introjection"[6], and when a person is carrying his own feeling and receives a further amount of this same feeling from another nearby person, so that the weight of feeling appears to be over-proportionate to the circumstances, whereas the other is apparently unmoved, we say he is experiencing a "double-dose". When a person carries a double quantity, the tension from the accumulation of feeling is enormous, and unless it can be released verbally in the hearing of another person who does not find it too frightening or too painful and who can be seen to hold it as if with his

4 There is, however, no general agreement on the definition of this term. Some writers use it in the sense that we do—of literally "putting out"; others define it as "attributing feelings to other people"; some use it in both ways.
5 and 6 Again there are differing definitions of these terms used in the literature.

own strength of consciousness, it often finds release in unfortunate and uncontrolled and apparently thoughtless actions which can bring harm to the person and those around him. This we call "acting-out".

These psychological mechanisms seem to be practised by all people, but more flexibly, and therefore less noticeably, by those with relatively well integrated personalities, who can allow themselves to react to situations where feelings of pleasure or pain seem to be inherent and appropriate to the facts. Because the feelings are not so overwhelming to the mind, they can be felt and expressed in privacy, or perhaps in semi-privacy, even if our particular culture does not allow their public expression as much as some others do.

These processes can be seen more easily in other people than in ourselves. Although they occur to a greater or lesser extent in all relationships, we can more easily distinguish them in a marital relationship. This potentially closest of adult relationships, with its socially acknowledged physically caring, loving and petting aspects, allows people to get as close as they will ever get, or can allow themselves to get, to the feelings they experienced as very young children in the first relationship they ever had.[7] Then they learnt what it was like to be held and loved (or not loved) and petted and cared for physically. It was at this time that they first learnt to use their ability, probably genetically evolved, to project, and then to project and to identify. Because it is always easier to follow the actual learned process than to try out something new, and because most children are reared in one family group whose adults already practise well established individual patterns of these mechanisms, able to hold some feelings but not others, the initial learning is usually continuously reinforced throughout childhood; a reactive pattern is established. Many situations can be described where one or other child has accepted a feeling from a parent who cannot express this for himself. For example, there is the adolescent who expresses not only his own bit of rebellion, which is part of the natural growth process of becoming more independent of his parents, but also, when his rebellion seems unnecessarily extreme, expresses that of his father who, to his cost, never dared to rebel at all.

7 See *Marital Tensions*. H. V. Dicks, Routledge and Kegan Paul, 1966. "I hope to show that marital bonds, both in health and in sickness, are the nearest adult equivalent to the original parent-child relationship. Projective identification, so prominent in the transactions of the marital dyad, belongs to the primary level of psychic function."

There are two reasons why projective identification is most clearly seen in marital relationships in our present-day English culture. The first is the degree of choice of partner which is allowed. As we become more geographically mobile and as more educational opportunity provides another leveller, it is becoming increasingly acceptable to take a partner from a wider range of people. Freer to find the person with the indefinable "It", with whom, or with which, we can fall in love, we are choosing someone who will fit psychologically, who will make us feel better and wholer, by providing an expression of the feeling we need them to feel for us. Secondly, the present-day small unit family, if not always educationally and vocationally many miles away from the two families of origin, at least often tightly boxed on a new housing estate or in a new town several miles away from parents and relatives, has to contain the whole range of emotions amongst a small group of people. Previously some of these feelings could be projected but retained amongst the aunts, uncles, sisters and cousins—the whole "extended" family—with whom day-to-day contact was maintained in the turning or alley.

These processes involved in the distribution of feeling between two people constitute a *folie à deux*. This is exhibited in any close relationship, but often the balance and complement in feeling, however much is projected or introjected, makes for a good and productive partnership at any one time. The continued ease of relationship, however, depends on the flexibility of the partners and on their ability to adapt to new circumstances, and to new roles, which they may have to perform and then to relinquish in the cycle of life.

The process of projective identification is most easily seen in marital relationships either where one partner cannot feel or express himself over a wide range of feeling, or where both partners with enormous persistence block off the opposite emotion to the one denied by the partner. (Emotions, as the emotional defences, can be paired off in opposites.) When the denial by one partner is so complete, the previously attractive characteristic in the other, now accentuated, becomes too much of a good thing, and leads to a degree of conflict which is more than the love can hold. Often neither partner can leave the other permanently, despite the fact that the varying ways in which they act-out appear to all onlookers to be destroying the confidence and the

47

ability of them both to do and to love appropriately. The non-feeler appears to be trying so hard to ease and to deal with the situation, yet underneath has a vested interest in maintaining the feeling in the other, even if he deplores the consequences.[8]

The reason for the gross denial of the emotion and the need to retain it in another person in adult life can often be seen in the broad outlines of the person's childhood; sometimes a deprived and painful childhood in which he had little practice of loving and being loved, so barely knows how to do it himself; sometimes a situation of once having experienced a loving relationship and then having lost it, so he dare not try again for fear of the pain of similar loss; or a childhood in which he was never allowed to be himself, or so spoilt or sheltered that he was never allowed to experience his own or other people's anger or learn how to deal with and hold his own frustration. But even if the way a person learnt to project so adroitly cannot be remembered or learnt from a social history, the continued practice of the learned pattern of what to project and what to introject can be seen in many disturbed marriages and families, and in the relationship with the worker. In a given situation where we would normally expect to find a particular and appropriate feeling common to the human beings concerned, and where we find one person apparently overcome by this feeling, and the other apparently unable to tolerate it, there is evidence to suggest that this mis-assortment of feeling is the work of the projective and introjective mechanisms.

Although Mr and Mrs Lorenz managed well in some areas of their lives they did have their distinct problems, which affected the distribution of feeling within their relationship. Through the course of a brief span of work they learnt to share these feelings' a little more appropriately. This in its turn enabled them to make a slight shift in their pattern of day-to-day living and decision making. Life generally became more comfortable for them. It certainly was still far from perfect.

Although the old pattern of feeling and behaviour had created a great deal of tension and difficulty, the prospect of change terrified them even more. Mrs Lorenz told Miss B. very clearly that she was expecting too much of her in too short a time, and

8 Teruel and Dicks support this "concept of one spouse 'carrying' or acting as the container of the other's internal object or objects, which the latter cannot contain". H. V. Dicks, *op. cit.*, G. Teruel, "Recent Trends in the Diagnosis and Treatment of Marital Conflict", *Psyche,* **20**, No. 8.

that she was not getting enough practice. The interviews, however, gave them some time to confirm themselves in a relationship with a worker who tried to remain relatively stable and dependable in her reactions, and with whom they did not have to maintain a social relationship outside the Institute. Any feelings which they were not yet able to retain in their own custody could be left there for the time being. The discomfort of learning could temporarily be forgotten. Again Mrs Lorenz was the one who put this into words when she explained how she forgot what went on in the interview until the day when she was due to come. Even after the first interviews, however, they did not forget completely and they took back into their home situation something about the need to know and to share knowledge, which had to be part of the change. They found a photograph which showed what Mr Lorenz looked like when he was twenty-one. It was a tentative first step which proved not to be disastrous. It is interesting that Mr Lorenz kept the beard, a physical symbol of the past, throughout most of the course of the work.

Some of what they established in the interviews with their workers they were able to confirm together at home. Mr Lorenz had talked more truthfully about his mother with Mrs A., and found that, despite the strength of feeling, this was all right; he was then for the first time able to do this with his wife—when he was in the bath. The bath was apparently safer than the sitting-room or bedroom. Perhaps the new standard of cleanliness, which is often equated with goodness in the unconscious, held the re-exposure of difficult and bad feeling, as Mrs. A had done. The exact emotional significance to him is not important. What was important was a new type of sharing and mutual acknow-ledgment of feeling. Later they were able to try even bigger experiments in their sharing pattern and carry it over into action. Mrs Lorenz was able to let Mr Lorenz plant the bottle garden for her. Although it was imperfect and not comparable with the ones on display in the shops, as her marriage still did not come up to the ideal she treasured in her fantasy life, the plants survived, despite the rough handling.

Helpful to Mr and Mrs Lorenz, while they were trying out new sharing patterns, was the ritualism of domestic living. Although at times they were muddled and ill at ease when they started to relinquish a long established method of relating to each other, they still had to face one another over many of the mundane, daily tasks which still had to be done. Feeling (and the expression of feeling) needs containment, particularly during a period of crisis, when these feelings are heightened or being newly felt and experienced. (For example, compare the allowed, open expression of grief behind the black veil, contained within the ritualism of a French funeral, with the "decent" reserve and stiff upper lip displayed at the simpler English ceremony.) Married life in its own right provides a most suitable container, or stabiliser, which supports that provided by the interview structure. This may be one of the reasons why work focused on the marital relationship often seems to be more effective in brief casework than that directed on other symptoms of personality disorder. The on-going marriage confirms the changing partnership and at the same time assigns, "roles and tasks to *each individual* by which he can recognise himself."[9]

At one point, when Mr Lorenz was very muddled, he became impatient that too much got left behind at the Institute and not transferred back into the relationship with his wife. In practice, however, the joint interviews achieved very little. This could be explained by their finding it more difficult to reveal their difficulties of interaction in public, as opposed to their examining them in private with one worker. Or it could be explained by the lack of skill of the workers, although both had had some, but not a great deal of, experience of joint interviews. In the first joint interview the shared projection of Mr and Mrs Lorenz in their denial of the need to tell and know about his borstal and prison sentences got into the workers, who felt frustrated and useless, particularly when Mr and Mrs Lorenz detailed their plans for escaping to Austria. The first joint interview was probably held too soon, as it was after this that Mr Lorenz really rejected Mrs A. as a person, trying to make her into a machine and to manipulate her as an object in his crisis of leaving the Institute.

In these experiments and in the process of slight shift and change, Mr and Mrs Lorenz sometimes swung too far over. When Mrs Lorenz learnt to accept and hold her own feelings about sex, she then saw the difficulty as being *all* her fault. The problem, however, was still mutual. He had expressed his difficulty several times to Mrs A. and she still did not cease to like him; "Am I all right or am I a queer?"; he had been a ladies' hairdresser, but now he was trying to be different; people expected him to be passionate, but really he thought he was a cold man,

9 *Insight and Responsibility.* E. Erikson, Faber, 1966.

who needed only infrequent sex. Their sexual behaviour, like their other difficulties, reflected their mutual inability to allow themselves to get close and to know each other. "No preliminaries and no afters" is probably as good a way of not getting close to another person as any other way. Mr Lorenz talked about his need for only infrequent sex in the interview after he had hovered by the tube station, unable to come to the building on his own, because he was not sure if he could bear to get attached to Mrs A. The only alternative was "to hate" her. This interview was the same week that Mrs Lorenz had told Miss B. that she had withdrawn the projection and now knew the sexual difficulty was hers. His no longer holding the double-dose, and the consequent reduction of feeling, although it left him muddled, probably enabled Mr Lorenz to talk about it more directly than he had done before, when his allusions to the subject had been brief—either quickly passed over or delivered as a parting shot. Whether, when the feelings were more evenly distributed, they ceased to worry about their mutual lack of passion, or whether, when the sharing generally became much easier, the sex found a warmer and more satisfying level, the workers were not told. Sex was not mentioned again by either Mr or Mrs Lorenz.

In this instance what happened in one interview had some influence on what happened in the interview with the other partner. Many of these parallels can be seen in the two sets of interviews. Sometimes, however, they continued to split off certain emotions and deposit them in one or the other of them. It was usually Mrs Lorenz who told both workers through Miss B. that things were generally better, and she did this in the weeks when Mr Lorenz failed to appear. The only occasion when she failed to come and bring the goodness, he had to carry it and the workers learnt from him through Mrs A. that they were "working things out a little better."

However, although there were both parallels and splits in these two sets of interviews, the actual work with the two clients was in one way quite different, particularly at the beginning. Mr Lorenz was carrying an overdose of many feelings, which he felt to be dangerous and destructive. Once he had plucked up courage to come, and had warned Mrs A. that she might cease to like him when he told her the worst, he needed very little help to put them into words. Much of the work that Mrs A. did with him was to show that she was not afraid of these feelings—not even of his fear of madness. If they did not damage her, perhaps he might learn

51

that they need not be too damaging to Mrs Lorenz or to himself. They could be tolerated and held. Despite the fact that he did at times seduce her into being too protective, her holding much of the sadness for him and her staunchness throughout, particularly at the end of the work, when he was very punishing to her, was a new and apparently meaningful experience for him. When some of the projections were withdrawn by Mrs Lorenz, and he had only his own feelings to deal with, which were already made safer by the airing of them to Mrs A., she was able to help him explore these feelings in more detail, which made them safer still. He gave the salient facts of his history and his difficulties in the first interview, but the feelings surrounding the events and people were worked with and allowed to be felt in much more detail in subsequent interviews.

Mrs Lorenz, however, was not carrying enough of her own feelings. The work with her was to help her to take some of them back into herself, and Miss B. refused to believe that she was not capable of being disappointed; she refused to believe, sad as her childhood had been, that the feelings surrounding mothers were so painful that they had to be deposited totally in her husband; and overall she refused to believe that Mrs Lorenz could not know. The salient facts in her history which had started off this pattern of not being able to know did not emerge until later in the work. In the first interview she skipped through the retinue of mothers without a care. When she first expressed her own feelings of disappointment and "let-down", it was in terms of presents, not of love. When she first told of the deception that had been practised on her, it was Miss B. who let out a gasp, and said, "How awful." It seemed for a long time that although feelings were talked about, it was only Miss B. who felt them. For the first time Mrs Lorenz's voice cracked when she described the scene when she had screamed for three days. In the next interview she could at last express very much more realistic doubts about the difficulties of knowing of her husband's criminality. Miss B.'s very rough attempts to help Mrs Lorenz be aware of her own feelings, and then share the sadness of these with her, were helped by Mrs A.'s sharing the extra quantity held by Mr Lorenz. This eased some of the tension in him, which may then have made the prospect of taking back a bit more of her share less frightening.

The shifts and changes in this couple during this brief span of work were easier to see than in some other couples who cover the same processes with a more skilful and subtle veneer of social and intellectual "know-how". Mr and Mrs Lorenz acted-out in their appearance and in many of their actions in and outside the Institute.

Mr Lorenz first came to the Institute driven by his own panic and feelings of tension. He did not want to do something awful and go back to prison. The tension fortunately exploded verbally in the Institute rather than outside. He expressed an enormous amount of bad feelings, no loving ones, and could talk of his wife only in terms of her caring for him. In the second interview he looked very scruffy and like he described himself to have been in the past. His feelings were more of humiliation. He wanted to love Jean, "to make a fuss of her", but he could only take her presents. He was, however, becoming increasingly anxious about these interviews, arriving earlier and earlier each time. It seemed very clear that this was connected with his fear that Mrs A. would cease to like him. Yet, when he arrived one hour early, he was so confused that he could not remember at the reception desk whom he wanted to see. Although his esteem of himself, reflected in his smarter appearance, seemed a little higher, the whole of the next two interviews went into greater detail about his anger with himself and with other people, particularly Mrs A. The second of these enabled him to acknowledge and express directly in words some of the deepest fears about himself, which previously he had only been able to express indirectly in his behaviour; anger and tenderness had to be kept apart. Then he did not come for two weeks. Just as he only felt in touch with his wife when he was angry, was this the only way he could keep in touch with Mrs A? These interviews released and perhaps contained the destructiveness inherent in the strength of his anger, allowing more room for affection and feelings of worth. If his anger had propelled him to the interviews, he may have had less impetus to come. Or he may have become so used to perpetuating relationships on an anger basis that he may have been fearful as to what would be left for him, if he could no longer rely on this same pattern of behaviour.

The next time he came he acted-out the new muddle he seemed to be in; he hovered round the tube station until Mrs A. found him. He was muddled about jobs and he was muddled about his feelings. He could no longer just hate, but getting close to people was still very painful for him. The anger was less, but he could not deal with the feelings of love. He then found a way of solving this and came nearer to being more comfortable with Mrs A. by projecting the hate on to Miss B. He was still very muddled, however, and could not hold the mixed feelings for Mrs A. when she was out of sight. His failure to behave more lovingly on Father's Day was accentuated by his having recently realised greater capacity to love, and to respond to love. Although the work had helped to reduce some of the anger, it had made life more painful for him in another, more grown-up way. Right to the end of the work he managed the duality of love and anger by splitting them off on to separate persons, the "good godmother" and the "bad grandmother", Mrs A. and Miss B. He was never able to express directly to Mrs A. his anger against her, the good mother, for leaving him, but was only able to act this out in the final crisis of not being able to tell. In his final individual interview with Mrs A., however, he seemed in many ways to be slightly more mature. Although he was almost, we might say, cruel to Mrs A., and his feelings seemed to be split, like his bosses, between three countries, he was more appropriately concerned about what being a new Hans might mean, and whether he could maintain the ground he had made in twelve weeks. Certainly in appearance he looked very much better; spruce, shaven and in a clean white shirt.

When Mrs Lorenz came for her first interview she showed surprisingly little sign of strain. Yet the circumstances she described —almost too fluently—indicated that she should have looked a little worried, a little on edge, or even slightly distressed. Although she continued to come for interviews, she later made it explicit that the interviews caused her pain. She did not look so well. As she took some feelings back nearer herself, they settled temporarily in her health, which deteriorated. Her thyroid was more unstable and she could hardly get up in the mornings when she came for an interview. It was only after she had consolidated the withdrawal and had become more accepting of her own feelings about sex, that she regained her powers of concentration and began to feel better. Her own words best describe the effect when a projection deposited in an owned person is finally withdrawn; "I have discovered that I can let Hans go. Before, I felt when he went away that only half of me existed." In a later interview she said, "In the past I have lived in and through Hans, despite his difficulties. When he was away working, I was not able to leave the house."

These new feelings and understandings, however, happened at the same time that Hans, who previously could not stand the noise of the linguaphone records, even though he bought them for her and ostensibly wanted her to learn German, was now hearing her pronunciation in the bath. It was a different sort of feeling, a different sort of sharing and a different sort of knowing. In one of the last interviews she and Miss B. spent some time discussing how much she should *choose to know* about her husband's business. In the last two interviews, however, when she was ambivalent about leaving the Institute, when the circumstances at home were in a state of crisis, when she did not know if they were moving to Austria or not, and when she did not know if she might be on the point of separation from her husband, she looked a mess. Her hair became increasingly untidy in the interview, as she repeatedly ran her hands through it, and her face, no longer bland, showed some of the immediate stress. Her clothes even became a little ruffled. She looked a little older, but much—much more real.

When looking at some of the features of the organisation of practice in the Institute in this second part of the discussion, we can ask the question whether Mr and Mrs Lorenz could be helped in this way by a field worker. The answer to this question is undoubtedly, "YES, they could be."

This answer does not mean that the case would be worked in exactly the same way. The reader was probably saying to himself as he read through the interviews, "Why did she not take up this? What a pity she missed that, and I wonder why she concentrated on this rather than that." Not only can cases be understood diagnostically according to different theoretical models, but they are worked in different languages—preferably those of the clients. Mr and Mrs Lorenz both had had a secondary modern education. They were quick learners; Mrs Lorenz, in her identification with Miss B., took over some of her language; and Mr Lorenz after only five interviews was able to recognise his wife's attempt to play the game of "Uproar"[10] when he wanted sex. Although we understood the work in terms of the mechanisms we have called projection and projective identification, it is unlikely that either Mr or Mrs Lorenz would now know what these terms mean. They were not used with them. When this case was presented for a discussion on marital work in a field department, one of the first questions to Miss B. was "Why did you not work with the latent homosexuality of this couple?" The answer is that the work was about latent homosexuality, but in the interviews it was called, "not feeling sexy" or "finding it difficult to share with your husband."

10 *The Games People Play*. E. Berne. Deutsch. 1966.

No two workers will ever use the same words, just as they will never feel exactly the same about two clients. Their hearing, their awareness, their acceptance, or non-acceptance, of feelings will always be different according to their own feeling experience and toleration. They will always use this hearing and themselves in slightly different ways and with varying degrees of consistency, confidence and conviction, intellect and emotion, skill and subtlety. They will also have their deaf and blind bits of feeling, which will prevent them hearing their clients in this same area.

There will, however, be some similarities in the work, whoever is the worker. These similarities will be based on the consistency of Mr and Mrs Lorenz's behaviour patterns, her adriotness at projecting certain feelings and his ability in accepting them. Flexibility in relating appropriately in different circumstances is often held to be a mark of maturity. It is certainly true that the more disturbed a person is, the more consistently his behaviour acts-out the same pattern, regardless of circumstances or of the reactions of other people, just like a needle caught in one groove on the gramophone record.[11] It is likely that most workers would have felt the frustration and have been over-persistent in response to Mrs Lorenz's consistent behaviour pattern, and it is likely that most workers would have had a tendency to over-protect the consistently childish Mr Lorenz. Many workers of average ability would have found it difficult to withstand his final attempts to manipulate, as did Mrs A. and Miss B., unless well supported within their working organisation.

One of the supports found in the Institute is the structured use of two workers rather than one. This enables the transference of feeling to be checked. When it was known through Miss B. that Mrs Lorenz had to protect her husband to the extent of not believing an authentic television programme, Mrs A.'s feelings of over-protection towards Mr Lorenz could be understood as part of the defences operating in the interaction, and not as solely part of her own nature. That she accepted the projection and found it so difficult to withstand was the strength of the feeling, accentuating that part of herself, which in moderation enabled her to be a good social worker. Although she knew she was behaving out of character, measured against her usual reactions, it was reassuring to know that Mr Lorenz forced his wife into behaving this way and that this piece of interaction was part of the problem.

11 Peter Brooke exemplified this in his direction at the Aldwych Theatre of the *Marat Sade*.

She was even more reassured when she saw Miss B. do exactly the same thing in the joint interview. Similarly Miss B. was reassured when she learnt that her disappointment, frustration and persistence in relation to Mrs Lorenz were not peculiar to herself. The two workers were able to make some use of their own feelings as a diagnostic check, but at the same time they did not have to be too concerned that their own reactions were at fault.

It can be argued that this type of information can be more economically picked up in a joint interview with only one worker. The transference of feeling to the worker is, however, usually heightened in a strong, one-to-one relationship, which the client feels he has for himself and which he does not have to share. His interaction with his partner can be more readily experienced by the worker in this situation. The number of clients per worker often reduces the investment of feeling by the same amount, unless they are all together projecting the same emotion; multiplied by two, three or four, it barrages the one worker with feeling. But if the clients are not all using the worker as a recipient for the same feeling, they can distribute their emotions around, and then the worker, not feeling them himself, has to make a guess at what they are. This is not always too difficult, as the feeling that would normally be aroused in such a situation can be used as a guide. The worker has, however, no idea of the strength, and when many different projections of feeling are crossing and criss-crossing round the room, some landing in him, some not, it is often difficult to pick out those on which he should be focusing the work.

Work with couples who are very out of touch with reality can perhaps only be done at first in a family situation; in individual interviews it is difficult to keep a sense of reality and to reconcile the two opposing perceptions of the situation. With relatively mature couples the work can probably be done on an individual or a family basis; different benefits may ensue, which may be equally valuable. During the present vogue for family therapy, however, it would be a pity to fail to recognise that some clients have a small amount of trust which they can consolidate in a tight one-to-one relationship and subsequently use in relationships with other people, but not enough to hold and use initially in a larger gathering; their precarious trust is so threatened that everyone seems to be against them, and they are unable to hear, feel or benefit from the workers' interventions. Mr Lorenz seemed to exemplify this state of emotional development, and was better helped by Mrs A.'s more obvious protection in the one-to-one situation. As yet the evidence from work in the Institute and other clinics is only suggestive, and not conclusive, as to when individual, joint or family interviews are best used.[12] The debate continues and we do not know the answer.

However, if it is easier to recognise the projections in one-to-one situations, if another worker provides a diagnostic check, if this diagnostic check gives additional strength and confidence to the two workers, if both partners can work more quickly when the resistance to change and fear in the other partner is also receiving attention, why do workers in the field not hunt in pairs more often?

Is this way of working too expensive? Is the expense justified, or not justified? At present we are without long-term, follow-up studies. Until these are available our estimates of expense and economy depend on values—values of long-term community mental health—and faith—a faith which has to last over many years, particularly if the client is a child, before the results can be known. Only when the children of the marriage in their turn marry and either make, or fail to make, appropriate and flexible close relationships, can the long-term value of the work be more accurately gauged. Any success with Mr and Mrs Lorenz may perhaps be measured by Mr Lorenz not having to go to prison again, after an explosion of inner tension in an act of assault, or by their better financial management, or by what they say they feel about themselves. Many years, however, will pass before Gerda chooses to marry either a stable, loving husband, or one who over acts-out his own and her feelings, because having taken her pattern of behaviour from her mother, she too cannot allow women to have feelings. If this work is effective for Gerda as well as for her parents, then we believe the expense was more than justified.

Too much money is, however, undoubtedly wasted in social work. Too much salary money is wasted chasing too many clients, over too long a period, with too long a gap between meetings. Too much of the good work done in one interview is wasted and lost, when not consolidated in a time span which is meaningful to the client. The worker may think in terms of monthly salaries, even of three months' notice, and may plan to get married or

12 See "Indications and Contra Indications for Conjoint Family Therapy". A. C. R. Skynner. *International Journal of Social Psychiatry*. Vol. 15. No. **4**. 1969.

change his job a year in advance. Many clients feel, think and plan only by the week, and sometimes cannot even do that—three days to go until the family allowance is due, four children to feed, and 13p. in the purse. An interview a month later, even if it is appointed, is quite beyond their feeling, as opposed to their intellectual, comprehension. It is not surprising that perceiving no further help in sight, nor more appropriately structured acknowledgment of the willingness to share and support them through the difficult process of expected change, they "forget", and make little progress.

The value of reduced caseloads, so meaningfully called "loads" (why not lists?), is obvious. Large caseloads do, however, have their uses and can protect workers from the disturbance of their clients.

A consideration, as important as that of reduction in size of caseload, is that of organisation, priority and the planned use of time. This is even more important the larger the caseload. There is an inspectoral element in statutory work which necessitates some clients remaining on the list. A watching brief has to be maintained, and for a period the maintenance of the Court Order may be beneficial to the client. Certainly workers cannot ignore the legislative rules. But case lists have swollen in size appreciably, despite the increase in staff, since concepts of community mental health and preventive work have been promoted. It is probably in this area of work that more skilful use of time can be made. Work distributed amongst fewer clients at any one time and more intensively directed during the periods of their crises, but not indefinitely, is probably far more effective in its results than when twice the number of clients are served less intensively over double the time. No fewer clients are served in the long run. Mr and Mrs Lorenz were offered help—weekly interviews—over a defined period of twelve weeks. The two workers both felt that this limitation of time, of which they were continuously aware, made them work very hard during the interviews. Mr and Mrs Lorenz both made a great deal of use of this time, and during this period they learnt a new way of looking at and understanding their own behaviour. There is no reason to suppose that they cannot continue to use some of these insights, although not all of them. We are not suggesting that twelve weeks was long enough for them to consolidate these changes. Ideally they should have had a longer period of help and support. We are also very much aware that the gains would have been greater if we, the workers, had had more skill.

Brief casework demands more professional competence than that which is prolonged over years.

Mr and Mrs Lorenz were certainly upset by the withdrawal of the workers, and their increased, anxious acting-out, which displayed that they still had many problems, was interpreted to them in these terms; but the value of the workers explicitly saying to them at the beginning that they thought twelve weeks would be long enough, of their acknowledgment of the continuing problems, and of their faith that Mr and Mrs Lorenz could now manage on their own, and yet of an open invitation to come back at another crisis point, cannot be gauged and must be left to the reader to estimate.

The emphasis here was put on "crisis". As Caplan [13] has stated, "Intervention directed towards ensuring a healthy outcome to an emotional crisis must operate at the time of acute disequilibrium in order to achieve maximum effect." A person's behaviour patterns may have "got him by" for a considerable period of time. Although uncomfortable, it probably has not been uncomfortable enough for him to want to undergo the temporary pain and anxiety that are involved in change. A crisis of accentuated feeling of not being able to manage, brought about by additional factors of external or inner stress, increases the motivation for change which is necessary if help of this type is to be effective. Change requires a slight shift in personality—a shift in the use of the mechanisms of projection and introjection which have been used in one particular way, often unwittingly, for many years.

In a study of "Brief Psychotherapy" [14] Malan found that "a high initial positive component of motivation both to come and for insight, or a marked increase in motivation following exposure to an interpretative situation, is a necessary condition to a score of 3 for outcome." (Patients were scored from 0 to 3 for outcome.) The inclusion of the phrase "and for insight" is important, as the patient must want the kind of treatment that is offered, if he is to benefit from it. He may not know initially what "treatment" means, but the initial interview should in fairness show him what it will mean.

This quotation is probably as relevant to the clients of social workers. Forgetting the technical words of "insight" and "interpretative situations", at least we could say, "*If a client does not*

13 *An Approach to Community Mental Health.* G. Caplan. Tavistock. 1961.
14 *Brief Psychotherapy.* D. H. Malan. Tavistock. 1963.

feel uncomfortable enough to want to change and to use the type of help that is offered to him, if he cannot temporarily tolerate a different type of pain and muddle, the outcome of brief casework is likely to be unfavourable."

Mr and Mrs Lorenz apparently did not have enough motivation when they were first referred. Two months later, however, Mr Lorenz could not tolerate his strength of feeling any longer. He did not want to do something "awful" and go back to prison. We can presume from this remark that he was aware that he *might* "do something awful." Mrs Lorenz was blatantly near to knowing. Despite her feeling uncomfortable when Miss B. said, "Why don't you want to know?" she accepted the offer of further appointments for a limited period with great alacrity. It is interesting to surmise whether she would have been so keen if no time limit had been set.

The motivation of Mr and Mrs Lorenz, however, dropped off, like that of most clients, after the fourth interview in his case and after the third in hers. He missed two interviews at this point, she missed one. The two workers expressed their concern about this in their discussions and wondered what these absences meant. As students they were attending lectures and had time to read. The current book or theory sometimes helped them to make sense of what they could not understand in their practical work. Malan figured at this time. Both of them felt better when they remembered that he had noticed there was a "remarkable prevalence of a decrease in motivation in sessions 3 to 5,"[15] not only in patients with whom the outcome of treatment is poor, but also with whom it is good. To consolidate this, Miss B. went in search of the book and read out to them both Malan's quote of Vosburg.[16] "In the first three hours (i.e. interviews) an initial history of the patient is taken, and the patient invariably reacts to his disclosures with strong feelings. Apparently because of these feelings, two-thirds of the patients either cancel or are late about the third interview. It would seem that this development is an initial crisis of psychotherapy." Supported by Vosburg as well as Malan, Mrs A. and Miss B. felt even better and thought they might surmount this "initial crisis."

As Dr J. D. Sutherland has said, "There's nothing so practical as a good theory." Theoretical backing gives enormous support to the workers, whatever the type of work. Training, which

15 *Ibid.*
16 R. L. Vosburg. "Some remarks on psychotherapy as reflected in hospital charts". *Psychiatric communications of The Western Psychiatric Institute,* University of Pittsburg, **1**, 151. 1958.

includes the acquiring of relevant knowledge, has supportive value. But we might well ask how far the motivation of the workers also falls off at this time. Although they were not conscious of it then, it seems that Mrs A.'s and Miss B.'s did this. One week they did not find time to discuss the interviews, and they delayed longer than usual in writing up the records, which suddenly became briefer. And the same thing seemed to be reflected in the discussion about this script. When they discussed the draft for the first three interviews, they remembered easily, they worked hard and they covered the work in a relatively short time. The fuller recordings made this easier. As they talked, the life of the case came back to them and they could easily feel themselves back into the parts they had played. But it became a struggle to do this on the fourth and fifth interviews, when one of the couple had missed an appointment. Desperately they wondered if their own lassitude was the effect of too big a lunch, or a reflection of the feeling in the work at that time.

Probably the motivation of the worker in wanting to help and the amount of his activity, whether this be in a doing or a talking or a feeling capacity, is as important a factor as the desire of the client to change his situation. A really actively attentive interview, even when little is said, is tiring. A defined time span and more closely spaced interviews may also be important for the worker in helping him to retain his interest at a level which ensures his continued activity.

The most important factors, illustrated in this record and discussion, which we believe were helpful to this type of work, can be summarised:

> The structured use of two workers on one case, each client having his own worker:
> A direct response to a crisis in the life of the clients, when the motivation for change is increased:
> The structured use of time as regards limit and weekly spacing, which helped to maintain the continued motivation and activity of both clients and workers:
> The use of a theoretical model, sometimes abstracted and simplified as in this paper, from which student-workers were helped to choose a focus of treatment and from which they were given "practical" support.

Certainly the workers benefitted, but, no less important, the clients did so too.

The Institute of Marital Studies

The aims of the Institute of Marital Studies are threefold:

(1) To offer a therapeutic service to those experiencing disturbance in their marriage.

(2) To develop the scientific understanding of the dynamics of interpersonal relationships as they are revealed in marital difficulties.

(3) To evolve methods of training other professional caseworkers in the handling of marital problems in ways appropriate to their own particular clinical settings or fields of social work.